MIX
Papier aus verantwortungsvollen Quellen
Paper from responsible sources
FSC® C105338

Winnie Waweru

Trends and impacts of China's FDI in Kenya

Anchor Academic
Publishing

Waweru, Winnie: Trends and impacts of China's FDI in Kenya, Hamburg, Anchor
Academic Publishing 2016

Buch-ISBN: 978-3-96067-092-6
PDF-eBook-ISBN: 978-3-96067-592-1
Druck/Herstellung: Anchor Academic Publishing, Hamburg, 2016

Bibliografische Information der Deutschen Nationalbibliothek:
Die Deutsche Nationalbibliothek verzeichnet diese Publikation in der Deutschen
Nationalbibliografie; detaillierte bibliografische Daten sind im Internet über
http://dnb.d-nb.de abrufbar.

Bibliographical Information of the German National Library:
The German National Library lists this publication in the German National Bibliography.
Detailed bibliographic data can be found at: http://dnb.d-nb.de

All rights reserved. This publication may not be reproduced, stored in a retrieval system
or transmitted, in any form or by any means, electronic, mechanical, photocopying,
recording or otherwise, without the prior permission of the publishers.

Das Werk einschließlich aller seiner Teile ist urheberrechtlich geschützt. Jede Verwertung
außerhalb der Grenzen des Urheberrechtsgesetzes ist ohne Zustimmung des Verlages
unzulässig und strafbar. Dies gilt insbesondere für Vervielfältigungen, Übersetzungen,
Mikroverfilmungen und die Einspeicherung und Bearbeitung in elektronischen Systemen.

Die Wiedergabe von Gebrauchsnamen, Handelsnamen, Warenbezeichnungen usw. in
diesem Werk berechtigt auch ohne besondere Kennzeichnung nicht zu der Annahme,
dass solche Namen im Sinne der Warenzeichen- und Markenschutz-Gesetzgebung als frei
zu betrachten wären und daher von jedermann benutzt werden dürften.

Die Informationen in diesem Werk wurden mit Sorgfalt erarbeitet. Dennoch können
Fehler nicht vollständig ausgeschlossen werden und die Diplomica Verlag GmbH, die
Autoren oder Übersetzer übernehmen keine juristische Verantwortung oder irgendeine
Haftung für evtl. verbliebene fehlerhafte Angaben und deren Folgen.

Alle Rechte vorbehalten

© Anchor Academic Publishing, Imprint der Diplomica Verlag GmbH
Hermannstal 119k, 22119 Hamburg
http://www.diplomica-verlag.de, Hamburg 2016
Printed in Germany

Abstract

Since China's reforms, the country has experienced tremendous growth and expansion, the China's government has encouraged the companies to go global, with the recent reforms of go west and global. Since China became a member of World Trade Organisation (WTO) in 2001 economic reform has been a spectacular economic success which has generated rapid economic growth over two decades and the country has moved from a centrally- planned economy towards a market economy. This dissertation will focus on the impact and the trends of Chinese FDI in Kenya's economic sectors in agriculture, infrastructure, manufacturing, and tourism. It seeks to quantify the advantages and disadvantages through the SWOT analysis and suggest policies necessary to maximize the development impact of China in Kenya.

This research study will take a qualitative and quantitative approach with close textual analysis of the existing data and information (from the Kenya embassy in Beijing and KIA) and auxiliary information from existing written literature, books, internet sources, journal articles and interpretation of the same existing literature materials.

Table of Contents

1. Introduction 5
2. Literature Review and theoretical background 8
   2.1 Kenya's strategic geographical location 10
   2.2 The Chinese business culture 10
   2.3 Availability of natural resources 11
3. Methodology 13
4. Results and Discussions 14
   4.1 Trends of the CFDI in Kenya 16
   4.2 Composition of the CFDI in Kenyan sectors 17
   4.3 Impacts of CFDI in Kenya; Model and SWOT analysis 18
      4.3.1 The model 18
      4.3.2 SWOT analysis 21
5. Conclusion and Policy recommendation 26
6. References 28
Appendices 31
   Overall CFDI (2014) 31
   Composition of CFDI in various Kenyan sectors 31
   Kenya GDP/Capita 32
   Interviews 33

Definition of terms

FDI   Foreign Direct Investment

EAC   East African Community

OECD   Organization for Economic Cooperation and Development

CFDI   Chinese Foreign Direct Investment

1. Introduction

Foreign Direct Investment (FDI) is an investment into one country by a company in production located in another state either by buying a company in the country or by expanding ventures of an existing business in the country.

FDI is made for various reasons, including taking advantage of cheaper wages in the state and special investment privileges, such as tax exemptions offered by the state as an incentive to gain tariff-free access to the local or regional markets.

Foreign direct investment contributes towards financing sustained economic growth over the long term. It is of particular importance for its potential to transfer knowledge and technology, create jobs, boost overall productivity, enhance competitiveness and entrepreneurship, and ultimately eradicate poverty through economic growth and development. In a similar vein, the OECD [OECD 2002a: 11] reckons that FDI has been recognised as a powerful engine and a major catalyst for achieving development, poverty reducing and global integration process. CFDI represents a great opportunity for Kenya and emerging economies to improve their balance of payments picture through increasing exports when investments are directed to the right sectors in the economy. The continent believes that China is keen to give assistance in technological skills transfer. On one hand, it is true that Africa looks at CFDI as a source to create economic growth and infrastructure development. On the contrary, China looks at this relationship as a prospect to help Africa with technology and capital to deal with these unexplored natural resources - not excluding China's needs to respond to the demand of raw material in Asian markets, including its local market. However, in the view of Carmody & Owusu (cf. Carmody & Owusu 2007), the Chinese model of development that is currently on offer is based on sophisticated technology, appropriate to African countries' low cost and expertise in poverty alleviation and SMME-small, micro and medium-sized enterprise development.

This model would allow African countries to have cheap access to new technologies and skills by enhancing local technological capabilities in all their economic sectors and their ability to compete in world markets. CFDI also brings technologies and knowledge that are not readily available to domestic investors, and in this way increasing productivity growth throughout the economy.

Chinese diplomacy in Africa, particularly the one that is carried out by the Ministries of Foreign Affairs and Trade has focused on bilateral relationships with African governments. Also, several State-owned banks have backed China's presence in Africa. China's Export-Import Bank (Exim Bank) that was established in 1994 to promote Chinese exports and foreign direct investment specifically in the infrastructure sector of roads, power plants, pipelines, telecommunications, among others [Wang, 2007]. The bank has a less risk-sensitive profile compared to private banks but is still more willing to support some investment projects than western counterparts. China Development Bank (CDB), also established in 1994 provides loans to Chinese firms and has launched the China-Africa Development Fund to support CFDI in Africa. Ever since 2001 SINOSURE (China Export and Credit Insurance Corporation) has been providing insurance against the risks involved in Chinese exports and foreign investment.

The China's growth and its capacity to progress from three decades of underdevelopment and extreme poverty, to an emerging global power and one of the largest exporter of manufactured goods, has attracted the attention of least developed countries. This advancement has led to China being a development model for Africa and an alternative source of trade and finance from Africa's traditional investment partners. The impact of Chinese investments in African economies has been diverse, depending on the sectoral composition of each country's production system. China's increased engagement with African countries have generated important gains for African economies. In this context, this study analyses the impact of CFDI in Kenya, quantifies the advantages and disadvantages through the SWOT analysis, and suggest policies necessary to maximize the development impact of China in Kenya.

The findings of this research investigation will be significant to the academicians, policy makers, and Chinese investors. It will also add knowledge and guide the researchers in this field of study.

2. Literature Review and theoretical background

Sino-Kenya relationship dates way back to 1964 when Kenya gained its independence, where China was the 4th country to recognise and congratulate her. Kenya and China have been trading partners since the Qing dynasty era and since the new millennium, CFDI has dramatically risen in different sectors of the Kenyan economy. One of the contentious issues surrounding Sino-Kenyan relations involves investments and bilateral agreements. In 2006, Kenya and China, through its leaders President Kibaki and his host President Hu Jintao, signed six agreements, signalling closer economic and technical ties between the two countries during a meeting held at the Great Hall of the People in Beijing. The signed agreements included economic and technical cooperation, agreement on the provision of concessional loans from China to Kenya and the Air Services Agreement, which grants Kenya Airways landing rights in several cities in China. In addition to this, since then Kenya was granted preferred tourist destination in 2004. Since then, the arrivals from China have doubled, and the numbers are expected to grow higher (cf. Kaplinsky R. et al., 2007).

Such initiatives have boosted the Kenyan economy by enhancing not just the earnings of the Airlines but also earnings for the tourism sector. Since March 2015, the Chinese Southern airline has been flying thrice in a week which facilitates and makes it easier for both, the Chinese and Kenyan business people to travel and has boosted tourism. These operations have a likelihood of facilitating the movement of Chinese business people to Kenya, resulting in increased foreign direct investment in Kenya from China (Onjala, 2008). Also signed were agreements on radio cooperation between the State Administration of Radio, Film and Television of China and the Ministry of Information and Communications of Kenya. A collaborative arrangement between General Administration of Quality Supervision Inspection and Quarantine of China and Kenya's Bureau of Standards was also signed (Kenya- Beijing embassy website).

Mega projects have been, and still are being undertaken in Kenya by the Chinese firms which will determine the future of the Kenyan economy and the growth of the CFDI in the country. These projects include hydropower plants, roads, and a multi-billion-dollar port in Lamu and the Southern Sudan–Ethiopia Transport Corridor (LAPSSET project) which includes a giant port for oil tankers, an oil refinery, pipelines from South Sudan and Northern Kenya, transportation hubs for rail, road and air vehicles. Some tourist resort cities are also expected along the development's path. Although Kenya has her traditional investors such as America, Japan and Europe, Chinese investors have increased in large numbers since 2002.

The theoretic background underpinning the FDI is presented by Dunning (1980) whose work is related to internalisation theory, identifies four basic economic motivations for firms or companies to enter a foreign market.

1) The search of new markets (market seeking)
2) The emphasis on efficiency of global markets (efficiency-seeking)
3) The search for strategic asset (strategic asset-seeking)
4) The search for new sources of resources (resources-seeking).

Buckley et al (2007) provide a good overview of the Dunning mentioned forms of FDI, stating that market-seeking FDI is undertaken by firms who are particularly keen to open up their good and services to export markets, but more particularly gain access to market that are showing signs of economic growth. Resource-seeking FDI takes place when firms seek to acquire or gain control of resources that are either not available or are in short supply in their domestic markets. Buckley et al (2007) indicated by the significant investments made by CFDI in countries with significant energy, oil, minerals and other raw materials. Efficiency-seeking FDI takes place when firms seek to reduce the cost of their operations and is commonly linked with firms from developed countries locating in developing countries to take advantage of low cost labour. Given the China's competitive advantage in attracting investors has always been associated with efficiency-seeking, it's unlikely that Chinese firms undertake FDI for efficiency seeking.

There are several factors in Kenya that influence the Chinese firms investing in Kenya. The factors include;

2.1 Kenya's strategic geographical location

As a member of the East African Community (EAC), Kenya has a strategic position in the region as the entry point to the Chinese FDI in the larger Eastern and Central Africa region, hence, there has been a rise of the CFDI through manufacturing and service sectors in Kenya. Infrastructure development has facilitated the movements of commodities within the regions. The Kenyan capital acts as the financial centre for the larger East Africa, with better developed facilities that enhances trade in the region.

2.2 The Chinese business culture

This has also contributed immensely to the Chinese firms investing in the country. Kenya, and Africa at large, see Chinese investors as friends/partners as opposed to other traditional investors who put so much political and economic conditions before in investing in a country. The Chinese policy of political non-interference increases their chance of investing in Africa. CFDI practice what is known as "coopetition" (simultaneous competition and cooperation) with global players both at home and in the host country. These ties with rivals sit well with the yin-yang philosophy that is so deeply rooted in Chinese culture: the yin (cooperation) and the yang (competition) can be seen as two mutually complementary sides of the same coin (Luo and Tung, 2007).

2.3 Availability of natural resources

According to Kogut (Kogut 1984) Chinese firms invest in Kenyan economy to extract raw materials, source production; or penetrate markets, and thus host countries need to provide this "bait" to lure Chinese investors to continue investing in their economy. Chinese firms investing in Kenya get comparative advantages, based on the location, due to lower factor costs, lower trade costs among others, so they can be said to be resource based investments due to resource availability. The Chinese interest in Kenya has also extended to mining and mineral exploration meaning that the sino-kenyan relationship is due to availability of resources in the East-African region.

Furthermore, the role of the government is a key facilitator and an aiding factor to the expansion of CFDI in Africa and other parts of the world despite the few restriction like limited experience in M&As, poor innovation process. China's presence in Africa also involves a broad range of private-sector actors, including multinationals, small businesses, traders, and migrants, as well as Chinese local governments, which at times act directly, mainly through the firms they own (Chen and Jian, 2009). While CFDI in Africa is likely to continue to be linked to trade, Kaminski and Morris consider that future CFDI will focus more on the private sector and the development of small and medium-sized enterprises (SMEs) in areas such as telecommunication, business services and manufactured goods(cf. Kaminski and Morris 2009).

China has given the priority to highly-visible, prestige projects, such as stadiums, highways, airports, and hospitals, making the African countries want to attract more CFDI. Foreign direct investment (FDI) not only provides the African countries with the much-needed capital for domestic investment but also creates employment opportunities, this helps in the transfer of managerial skills and technology, all of which contribute to economic development. Recognizing that FDI can play a major role in economic development, all governments of

Africa including that of Kenya want to attract the CFDI. Indeed, the global market for such investment is highly aggressive. Kenya, in particular, seeks such investment to accelerate her development efforts and achieve "The Vision 2030". The increase of China's commercial operations in Africa is arguably the most momentous development on the continent today. China encourages its businesses to import Kenyan goods, expand investment in Kenya, participate in its infrastructure construction and energy & resources exploitation and expand cooperation with Kenya in processing industries and agriculture. China will continue contributing economic aid within its available resources and intensify assistance for Kenya's human resources development (Onjala, 2008).

However according to a survey by World Development Report 2005, The World Bank shows that the Kenyan competitiveness to attracting more FDI has been on decreasing trend in the recent years. It should be noted that Kenya 's ability in attracting FDI is crucial as it serves a gateway to Eastern and Central Africa and hence she should be attracting more FDI than any region in Africa. This research calls upon other researchers to investigate and come up with more policy favourable to attracting the CFDI in the region, particularly in Kenya. In the following chapters, the main research focus will be the analyses of the impact of Chinese FDI in various sectors - mainly in the infrastructure, manufacturing, agricultural, and service industries - in Kenyan economy. With the reference to the last ten years. It will also delve into bilateral agreements that have been signed by the Chinese and the Kenyan governments

3. Methodology

This research study took a qualitative and quantitative approach, with close textual analysis of the existing data, as well as discussions which were conceived as qualitative expert interview (from the Kenya embassy in Beijing and KIA officials). Auxiliary information was obtained from existing written literature, books, scientific papers, journals and interpretation of the existing information and data.

The applied methodology approach sought to answer the three research questions stated below:

I. What are trends of CFDI in different sectors (agriculture, tourism, manufacturing, and infrastructure development)?

II. Are there positive or negative impacts of CFDI in Kenya?
Using the simple regression Model: GDP $(Y) = \alpha + \beta_0 X_0 + \beta_1 X_1 + \beta_2 X_2 + \beta_3 X_3$

III. What are the opportunities and threats of CFDI in the Kenyan economy?

This study posed some difficulties due to the biasness of the data and lack of real-time information. The existing data was not comprehensive, thus, the researcher was faced with difficulties in the interpretation of the results.

4. Results and Discussions

The data for this study was acquired from the Kenya Investment Authority (KIA), Kenya Beijing embassy 2014 data and interviews (Appendix D) with various experts providing a deeper understanding of the CFDI in Kenya. The types of CFDI are diverse they include; restaurants set-ups, car/motorbike or bicycle assembling, coffee or tea growing, toys manufacturing, cement manufacturing, road/ airports construction and real estate development among much more.

Table 1 – Types of CFDI 2014. Table by Kenya Beijing embassy

ACTIVITY	CAPCOST(F)	CAPCOST(L)	EMPLOYMENT(F)	EMPLOYMENT(L)	ISIC
Assembly of Motor Vehicles and Generators	20	0	1	66	SERV
Real Estate development	645	0	4	16	CONST
Market research and data collection	612.8	0	2	2	SERV
Cement manufacture	5800	0	100	500	MANU
Manufacture of gypsum product	272	0	13	125	MANU
Road construction	38400	0	5	200	CONST
Motorbike assembly	8	0	2	6	MANU
Manufacture of steel doors	570	0	28	105	MANU
Manufacture of security doors & hardware materials	2038	0	4	175	MANU
Processing & export of intestines	23.4	0	0	20	SERV
Assembly and Trading of machinery	170	0	6	37	SERV
Restaurant	8	0	6	20	TOUR
Manufacture of foods and beverages	109	0	5	65	MANU
Manufacture of dry cells	315	0	8	183	MANU
Import & wholesale of garments, textiles, toys	20	0	0	10	SERV

According to Kenya Investment Authority report 2014, most of the Chinese companies in Kenya are either fully owned by Chinese companies or are privately owned, hence very limited or no local capital. The capital cost is mainly foreign which is so much needed in the country. The foreign capital in 2014, averaged to 62231.28 (KSH in millions) and local capital of 726.05 (KSH in millions). With the capital extensive sectors like manufacturing and construction attracting the highest amount of foreign capital. In 2014 agriculture attracted the least amount of foreign capital and zero local capital. The construction and the manufacturing sectors attract the highest number of foreign employment which is primarily managerial positions hence the evidence of managerial skills transfer to the local Kenyan people. This is contrary to the popular "stories" that CFDI only hire the Chinese people in the host countries. In 2014 there was 11264 local employees and only 1077 foreign employees. ISIC indicates that the investments in 2014 were scattered in the sectors of manufacturing, service, tourism and construction, with service and manufacturing sectors offering the highest number of employment to the local people, hence improving people's livelihood.

4.1 Trends of the CFDI in Kenya

The data of this study covered a span of 10 years. Figure 1 below shows the trends of CFDI in the last decade from the year 2006 to 2015.

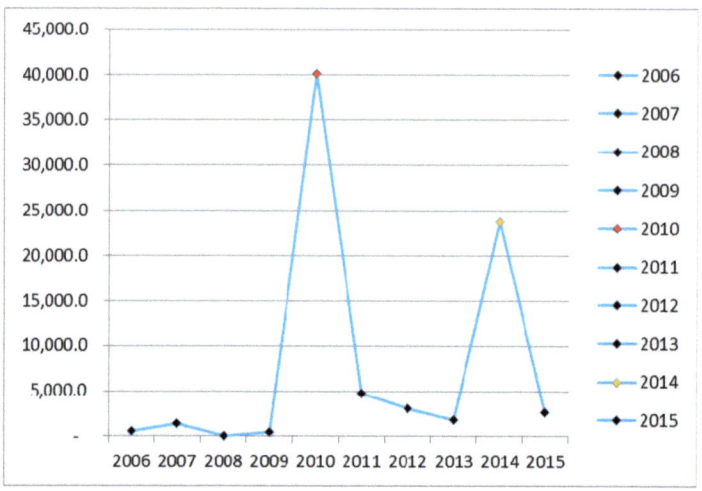

Figure 1 – The trends of CFDI in Kenya. KHS in million 2006-2015. Source of data: KIA

Kenya has been experiencing decreasing trends of the CFDI, due to different economic and political factors both internal and external factors. From Fig. it is true that the level of CFDI has been low and stagnant over a previous couple of years (2006-2008) and well below Kenya's potential. In 2008, it was even lower due to the impacts of the global financial crisis and the 2007/2008 post-election violence in Kenya. In 2009 and 2010 saw a sharp rise of CFDI as the economy recovered from the world financial crisis the signed bilateral trade agreements signed in 2006 took effect, followed by the passage of the new constitution, which stabilised Kenya politically. According to KPMG in "Africa Document Kenya", the promulgation of Kenya's new constitution in August 2010 put in place a framework to establish regulatory institutions that support investment growth and productivity (KPMG

2007). In these years, there was massive infrastructural construction including road, airports, shopping malls and most of the investment undertaken by the Chinese companies. In the period between 2011 and 2015, it was a dark period for the Chinese investments in Kenya. Since 2011, at least 135 Al-Shabaab attacks have been reported in Kenya (KIPPRA - Policy Monitor Issue 7). The terrorists' attacks from the Al-Shabaab created uncertainty and prevented potential investors from making new capital investments (Business Daily Africa paper, 2016). Terrorist attacks in the Kenyan economy have cost her to lose CFDI attractiveness. The attack in 21st Sept. 2013 on the Westgate Mall, an Israeli-owned investment, has seen some investors leaving Kenya to invest in other neighbouring countries, despite the Kenyan strategic geographical position as an entry to Eastern and Central Africa.

4.2 Composition of the CFDI in Kenyan sectors

The CFDI in Kenya has been directed in different sectors. The pie chart below (Figure 2) illustrates the results of the data of Table 3 (Appendix, Table 3 - Composition of CFDI in various Kenyan sectors).

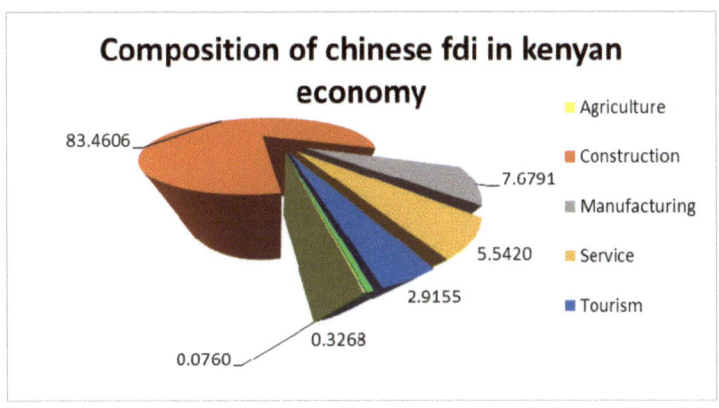

Figure 2 – Composition of CFDI in Kenyan economy. Source of data: KIA

Figure 2 shows that the CFDI is mainly concentrated in construction and manufacturing. Agriculture has received the least, with about 0.076% of the Grand Total Investments. The highest amount of the CFDI was directed in Infrastructural development, including construction of roads, standard gauge railways, stadiums, hospitals, shopping malls, airports and real estate development. The manufacturing sector is the second highest in attracting CFDI with about 7.6791 percent of the total CFDI and, has a great potential in assembling vehicles and cars, cement manufacturing, glass, food, beverages and dry cells among other products. Service and tourism industries have also attracted a substantial amount of CFDI of about 5.42% and 2.9155%, respectively - that includes restaurants, treatments, schools and the tourist arrivals in the country.

4.3 Impacts of CFDI in Kenya; Model and SWOT analysis

4.3.1 The model

GDP $(Y) = \alpha + \beta_0 X_0 + \beta_1 X_1 + \beta_2 X_2 + \beta_3 X_3 + \varepsilon$ this model was applied to determine how much CFDI contribute to the economic growth in Kenya. Linear regression equation was used to study the relationship between the GDP/Capita and the CFDI in various sectors of the economy.

Table 2 – Impact of CFDI in Kenyan sector. Source of data: World bank and KIA and Kenya Beijing embassy 2014

COEFFICIENTS [a]

Model		Unstandardized Coefficients		Standardized Coefficients	T	Sig.
		B	Std. Error	Beta		
1	(Constant)	838.902	85.208		9.845	.000
	Agriculture	11.560	2.733	.840	4.230	.008
	Construction	.002	.004	.113	.561	.599
	Manufacturing	.084	.069	.241	1.221	.277
	Service/Tourism	.166	.059	.574	2.824	.037

a. Dependent Variable: GDP/Capita

Y-GDP/Capita, α - Autonomous GDP/Capita, X_0-Agriculture, X_1- Construction, X_2-Manufacture, X_3- Service and Tourism and ε Error term.

The established multiple linear regression equation becomes; $Y = 838.902 + 11.560X_0 + 0.002X_1 + 0.084X_2 + 0.166X_3 + ε$

α = 838.902; shows if the CFDI in agriculture, construction, manufacturing, service and tourism were all zero, GDP/Capita will be 838.907.

X0 = 11.560, shows that 1unit change in agriculture results in 11.543 unit increase in GDP/capita.

X1= 0.002, shows that 1unit change in construction results in 0.002 increase in GDP/capita.

X2= 0.084, explains that 1unit change in manufacturing results in 0/084 unit increase in GDP/capita.

X3= 0.166 shows that 1unit change in service & Tourism results in 0.166 unit increase in GDP/capita.

All predictor variables X0. X1, X2, X3 i.e. the GDP/capita and CFDI in the economy has a positive relationship.

Table 3 – Overall impact of CFDI in Kenyan economy. Source of data: World bank and KIA

ANOVA[a]

Model		Sum of Squares	d.f	Mean Square	F	Sig.
1	Regression	501630.644	4	125407.661	5.590	.043[b]
	Residual	112176.185	5	22435.237		
	Total	613806.829	9			

a. Dependent Variable: GDP/Capita

b. Predictors: (Constant), Service/ Tourism, Manufacturing, Agriculture, Construction

The overall model $Y= 838.902+ 11.560X_0 + 0.002X_1 + 0.084X_2 + 0.166X_3 + \varepsilon$; is statistically insignificant as F=5.590 & P= .043[b.] All predictor variable agriculture, construction, manufacturing service and tourism i.e. GDP and CFDI in the economy has a positive relationship but statistically insignificant.

4.3.2 SWOT analysis

As the Chinese investments in Kenya have been experiencing a decreasing trend, this has simultaneously triggered more interest of the traditional Kenyan investors, such as Europe, America, Japan and so on in the areas of energy, agriculture, technology, energy among other (Appendix, Interview). This has helped the country to diversify and avoid over-reliance of one source of FDI. Diverse FDI sources acts as insurance against financial shocks (UNCTAD 2010). CFDI capital cost which in mainly foreign has spurred economic growth and development, not only in Kenya but also the Eastern Africa region. Infrastructure development which the Chinese companies have heavily invested in the country has eased transportation of the manufactured and agricultural products around the E.A. countries. Infrastructural development has also been a major reason why other investors have come on board as they find the country as an entry point to the larger East- and Central Africa markets. Continued investment in infrastructure is imperative to further lowering the production costs, which has transformed key sectors like agriculture, tourism and manufacturing (Figure 2). Investments in the real estate industry have led to more office space in the Nairobi, the economic hub of the region, hence it has facilitated the country to hold more world conferences like the recent Round 12 of the WTO. Such conferences brand Kenya as a premier destination for global meetings.

CFDI in Kenya is a major source of employment - especially in the manufacturing industry, which offers both skilled and unskilled labour. Most of the CFDI are labour intensive hence employs a lot of the local Kenyan.

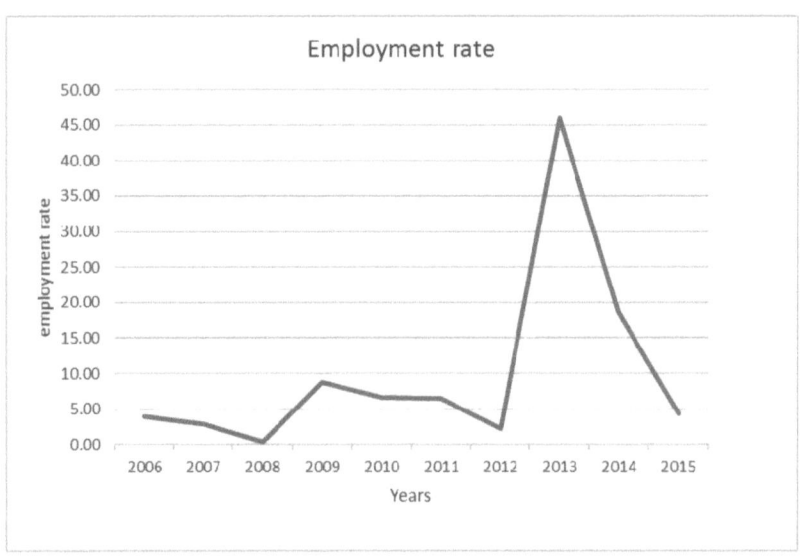

Figure 3 – Employment rate. Source of data: KIA on number of local employment – Kenya Beijing embassy 2014

According to table 2: Overall CFDI 2014 the total local employees was 11,264 people in all sectors and only 1077 foreign employees. In 2014 the manufacturing and service industries had the highest number of local employees of 6921 and 2958 respectively and foreign employees of 576 and 186 respectively. We can confidently say that the CFDI is a major employer in Kenya. Besides the source of employment which is highly sought, CFDI also has led to technological know-how spill over. New skills have been transferred to the Kenyan population. Chinese technical prowess has powered modernization and expansion of Kenya's transport infrastructure, particularly in rail, roads and air (Appendix, Interview).

Although the CDFI has been beneficial for the Kenyan economy, especially the non-debt creating resource capital, environmental issues remain a threat to the Kenyan economy, if the CFDI activities are not controlled in the country. In the recent past the NEMA (National Environmental Management Authority) has warned about the environmental pollution in areas where the factories and the manufacturing plants have been opened. The firms evade the installation of proper sewage facilities and costs. Instead, they drain the waste to the nearby water bodies. The CFDI firms lack the corporate social responsibility of environmental management and sustainability.

Consumers benefit from cheap products like the electronics, footwear& clothing among others. The quality of Chinese products in the country remains a hindering factor to the CFDI expanding in the country. A lot of Kenyans still believe Chinese goods are either fake or are of low quality, although they are cheap and affordable to many Kenyan households (Appendix, Interview).

Insecurity in the country and a hostile business environment have continued posing a threat to the Kenyan economy. The frequent terrorist attacks in the country make it impossible for investors to invest in the country. Furthermore, the recurrent travel bans to the country, especially in the tourist destinations, hurt the state of economy.

Macroeconomic factors like inflation and currency depreciation cause the state to lose FDI attractiveness, especially in manufacturing industries which entirely depend on energy for production. If the production costs increases due to inflation, the products become expensive and unattractive.

Technology is a double-edged sword - its' advancement has led to rising cyber-crimes, that is catastrophic, not just to individuals but also to the government agencies, institutions like banks and private investors. There are many cases of hacking especially in banks and data theft. Kenya has more to lose if IT securities are not prioritised, especially with the widespread popularity of new e-services by governmental agencies and e-financial services like M-pesa (Mobil money).

Agriculture is the mainstay of the economy and a major contributor of the Kenyan total export. Kenyan agricultural sector possesses a huge opportunity for the investors that include manufacturing of greenhouses and construction. There are well-established export markets for horticultural products (fruits and flowers), cash crops like coffee and tea, cotton and tobacco. Most importantly, there are bilateral agreements that favour local agricultural and manufactured Kenyan products (KIA 2016). Which the investors should cease the opportunity and invest.

The Kenyan aspiration to industries is gradually being realized with CFDI heavily investing in the manufacturing sector. According to the development blueprint Vision 2030, the core of industrialization is the vibrant manufacturing sector for value addition and sophistication. In the manufacturing industry the country possesses huge opportunities - both directly and indirectly investments (KIPPRA 2014). The local manufacturing companies have also improved efficiency or upgraded their standards to the international levels, helping the local companies compete globally. The cost of labour is favourable, and the Kenyan human resource is rich with skills. In fact, the country has the most skilled workforce in the region. CFDI can take advantage of the well-equipped human capital and the cheap labour cost to set up the manufacturing plants in the country

There has been a huge demand for the affordable housing in the country. The devolution system of governance in place has led to an increased demand for real estate development in the country. Each county in the country is competing to have modern, affordable housing for workers, schools, hospitals and other commercial and industrial infrastructures. Some counties offer free land for the foreign investors to invest in their counties. Devolution system of governance has created a huge opportunity for the investors to invest in various sectors and especially in agriculture and manufacturing sectors which have high return. Kenya also has potentials in the tourism industry and in environmental -natural resource areas. Due to the rise of the ecological tourism, the government encourages both local and foreign investors to invest in putting up eco-lodges, tree houses, guest houses, restaurants, campsites and canopy walkways (KIA 2016). Kenya is also endowed with rich industrial mineral resources and oil deposits along the coast and in the Northern part of Kenya.

Environmental conservation consultancy services are also required. Huge opportunities also exist in solid and electrical waste management. The country is developing at a very high rate but has no capacity to deal with the problems that emanate from such industrial development. The availability of cheap Chinese products in the economy also poses threats to the growth of the local industry in the country e.g. the indefinite closure of "Kenya Fluorspar Mining Company" in the Kerio Valley, that has been operational in the country for the last 40 years (Mwangi 2016). The local companies lack the competitive advantage for the Chinese imports in the economy.

5. Conclusion and Policy recommendation

The objective of this study was to determine the impact of the CFDI in the Kenya and if its positive or negative. The fact is that CFDI induces the nation's growth positively. The overall CFDI effect on the whole economy may not be significant this can be explained by the fact that there's low Chinese investment in agricultural sector which is the major Kenyan GDP contributor. The components of CFDI positively affect economic growth and should be encouraged. Kenya is well endowed with the arable land, and modern agricultural methods should be used in the production of agricultural products. Bilateral agreements have influenced growth of CFDI in Kenya and cooperation in other areas of the economy should be encourage for Kenya to industrialise faster. Proper policies should be created to attract more of CFDI as there many more investment opportunities existing in Kenya.

Kenya has been receiving low CFDI below its potential. Kenya can use the foreign diplomacy policies to market herself as the entry point to the larger Eastern and Central Africa. Rebranding Kenya as an entry point will help attract more sophisticated market-seeking CFDI in the country and simultaneously lead to improved infrastructures including modernisation of the ports, cheap transport and improved economic efficiency.

This study recommends first the Kenyan government should create investment friendly policies where the CFDI can operate for the country to yield maximum benefits of CFDI. The negative vices like corruption, political and policy instability which cripples the CFDI development should be dealt with comprehensively. Secondly, proper laws should be put in place to combat crimes, insecurity threats, and especially terrorist attacks, which negatively affect tourism and the service sectors. The cyber crimes which create insecurity to the financial and banking systems should be controlled by properly set up laws.

Thirdly this study recommends that the Kenyan stakeholders and negotiators should step up and negotiate for quality investments to the economy - those investments that do not pose harm to the local industries but give them room to expand and compete globally. The environment management and sustainability policies should be addressed as the Kenyan economy industrialises and moves to a manufacturing economy. There should be policies that favour the national interests e.g. food security, natural resource management while offering attractive offers to the CFDI.

The Chinese investors should also familiarise themselves with Kenyan labour laws and regulations. Many Chinese companies are faced with a lot of legal issues in Kenya. The court process is expensive and lengthy, causing delays to the proposed projects in the country.

The researcher recommends that more detailed and in-depth research on this topic of the impacts of CFDI in Kenya and East Africa at large; since the researcher had limited resources thus she did not delve into the subject.

6. References

Auboin, M. (2007). "Boosting Trade Finance in Developing Countries: World Trade Organization, Geneva.

Blomstrom, M, Kokko, A. (1998). "Multinational corporations and spill-overs", Journal of Economic Surveys, Vol. 12, pp. 24.

Business Daily Africa paper (2016). "What terrorist attacks are costing Kenya", April 9th 2016.

Carmody & Owusu (2007). "China versus American geo-economics strategies in Africa". 26, pp. 504-524.

Chen, Z., and Jian, J. (2009). "Chinese Provinces as Foreign Policy Actors in Africa", Occasional paper No. 22, South African Institute of International Affairs, Johannesburg.

Ernst & Young (2015). Kenya Daily Nation, July 27, 2015.

Gathaiya, R.; Kinyua, J.; Machuki, P.; Keraro, V. (March 2014). "The Impact of Foreign Direct Investments by Chinese Companies in Kenya", Jomo Kenyatta University of Agriculture and Technology (JKUAT), Nairobi, Kenya.

Jian-ye Wang (October 2007). "What drives china's growing role in Africa." IMF working paper we/07/2007, Authorized for distribution by Benedicte Vibe Christensen.

Kaplinsky RD, McCormick D, Morris M (2007). "The Impact of China on Sub-Saharan Africa", Working Paper 291, Institute of Development Studies, University of Sussex, Brighton.

Kaplinsky, R. & Morris, M. (2009). "Chinese FDI in Sub-Saharan Africa: Engaging with Large Dragons", the European Journal of Development Research, 21(4), pp. 551-569.

Ken Invest (2016). Opportunities, http://www.investmentkenya.com/opportunities, viewed 03/10/2016.

KIA (2016). Kenya Investment Authority, http://www.kenyaembassy.cn/content/content.aspx?kid=71, viewed 03/07/2016.

Kioko, P.M. (14th March 2012). "A study on Chinese economic relations with Africa. Case study, Kenya", Prime Journal of Business Administration and Management.

KIPPRA (July - December 2014). Policy Monitor Issue 7, No. 1.

Kogut, B., Singh, H. (1988) "The effect of national culture on the choice of entry mode", Journal of International Business Studies, Vol. 19, No. 3, pp. 411-32.

KPMG in Africa Document Kenya (2012) KPMG PDF page 15., https://www.kpmg.com/Africa/en/KPMG-in-Africa/Documents/Kenya.pdf, viewed 03/12/2016.

Kriel, R. (2015). "Kenya's Westgate mall reopens, nearly two years after bloody terror attack", http://edition.cnn.com/2015/07/18/africa/kenya-westgate-mall-reopens/, viewed 04/04/2016.

Lauren, J. (2015). "China's road to growth in Africa" East Asia Forum Economics, University of Melbourne - Politics and Public Policy in East Asia and the Pacific, 7th February 2015.

Luo, Y. and Tung, R.L. (2007). International expansion of emerging market enterprises: A springboard perspective, Journal of International Business Studies, 38/4, 481-498.

Motta, P. (2004). "To what extent can foreign direct investment help achieve international development goals?" The World Economy, Vol. 27, No. 5, pp.657.

Mwangi, B. (2016). "At least 100 to lose jobs as commodity prices fall", http://www.nation.co.ke/business/corporates/Kenya-Fluorspar-to-sack-100-workers-as-commodity-prices-fall/-/1954162/3082500/-/meg8ej/-/index.html, viewed 03/20/2016.

Ogalo, V. (2011). "Foreign Investment in Agriculture in Eastern Africa: A General Overview of Trends and Issues".

Olga Timokhina (2014). "Chinese foreign direct investment in Africa in corporate social responsibility context" working paper No. 2014/29.

Onjala J (2008). "A scoping study on China – African Economics Relations: the case of Kenya", African Economic Research Consortium (AERC), Nairobi, Kenya, 5th March 2008.

Quer, D.; Claver, E.; Rienda, L.(2007). "China's Outward Foreign Direct Investment: Driving Factors, Theoretical Background and Strategic Implication.

Appendices

Overall CFDI (2014)

Table 4 – Source: Kenya Investment Authority (KIA) 2014

ISIC	EMPLOYMENT L	CAPCOST F (KHS Million)	CAPCOST L (KHS Million)	EMPLOYMENT F
AGRI	301	607.04	0	18
CONST	540	43061	0	265
MANU	6921	12793.57	450.15	576
SERV	2958	3915.37	272	186
TOUR	544	1854.3	3.9	32
TOTAL	11264	62231.28	726.05	1077

MANU = manufacture; "SERV" = Service; "TOUR"= Tourism; "CONST"= construction/infrastructure; "CAPCOST F"= capital cost (foreign); "CAPCOST L"= capital cost (local); "EMP F"= employment (foreign); "EMP L"= employment (local).

Composition of CFDI in various Kenyan sectors

Table 5 – Source: Kenya Investment Authority (KIA) 2006- 2015

KSH Million										
SECTOR	2006	2007	2008	2009	2010	2011	2012	2013	2014	2015
Agriculture	-	-	-	-	-	-	-	-	-	60.0
Construction	-	-	-	454.0	39,600.0	3,045.0	-	-	20,898.0	1,901.4
Manufacturing	175.0	1,413.5	-	-	415.0	244.9	2,310.0	900.0	9.0	595.9
Service	370.6	15.0	46.4	-	155.6	355.0	816.2	640.2	1,968.8	8.0
Tourism	-	15.0	7.0	15.0	-	1,075.0	-	330.0	860.0	-
Wholesale and retail	-	-	-	48.0	-	40.0	-	-	73.0	97.0
Grand Total	545.6	1,443.5	53.4	517.0	40,170.6	4,759.9	3,126.2	1,870.2	23,808.8	2,662.3

These figures do not represent the cumulative number of investment projects registered in the country since the law does not require all investors to register (or at least submit information) with Ken Invest.

Kenya GDP/Capita

Table 6 – Created from: World Development Indicators. Series: GDP at market prices in million (current US$)

year	2006	2007	2008	2009	2010	2011	2012	2013	2014	2015
GDP	711.72	857.92	938.57	942.74	991.85	1012.88	1184.92	1257.20	1358.26	1588

Interviews

The following Interview was conceived as a qualitative expert interview. For reasons of confidentiality and privacy, all personal and source-specific data was anonymized. The interview partners are working as officials in relation with the Kenyan government.

Question 1: "What are the major impacts of CFDI in Kenya?"

1st Response:

"First and foremost the Chinese interest in Africa and in Kenya has triggered the interest of other investors from Europe, Japan, and India among others who want to invest in the country."

2nd Response:

"The CFDI has made products readily available and affordable to the local people. Chinese goods are cheap and affordable."

3rd Response:

"The CFDI has helped in infrastructure development e.g. the construction of roads, railways lines and airports have opened up the rural areas and making transportation of agricultural products and other commodities easier and easier. The roads infrastructural development in the capital has eased traffic jams hence increasing human productivity."

Question 2: "What is the future of CFDI in Kenya?"

"China will remain a strategic partner with Kenya as the East African nation implements an ambitious infrastructure and industrial development agenda. The CFDI will continue to have a place in Kenya especially with the new devolved system of governance. The newly created counties are competing to attract more FDI to invest in road, private and commercial real estates, better housing for their workers and other amenities like hospitals and schools.

The Kenyan aspirations to industrialize are being gradually by the CFDI investing in manufacturing industries and in Agri-business. With so many investing opportunities existing like mineral and oil explorations, energy resources, the CFDI will always be encouraged.

Moreover, the Chinese firms are more preferred as they offer their services more cheaply as compared to the other investors."

Question 3: "What are the risks/ threats of CFDI to Kenyan economy?"

"The CFDI has been of great benefit to the country. Kenya has realized most of its development goals. However, the local young industries face much competition from the Chinese firms, leading to a declining productivity because of lack of sufficient market and eventually shutdown their operations. Environmental issues also remain a threat. There have been reports that most of the areas where the Chinese industries operate/ located are highly polluted."

"The technological advancement is also a threat. There has been recent detention of the Chinese citizens in Nairobi (Kenya capital city) who committed cyber crimes like hacking in companies, security companies and stealing money in the banks."